The Egypt Book

Warfare by Duct Tape

DISCLAIMER AND TERMS OF USE AGREEMENT

ISBN-10:1942006004 ISBN-13: 978-1-942006-00-8

Table of Contents

Note about the Egyptians:
In The Egypt Book, the history and weapons of Egypt have been highlighted. The intent of this book is **not** to endorse or glorify the false gods, incorrect beliefs, traditions and culture of the Egyptians. In the end, God judged the Egyptians for these things. To read more of the story, see Exodus 2-11.

The Weapons

Short Sword

Straight swords were a rarity during the Bronze Age. Bronze as a metal is not very strong. Long bronze swords would quickly bend out of shape during use. That is why bronze swords were relatively short, particularly if they were straight. This weapon was effective for both cutting and thrusting. This would be a weapon among the well-to-do Egyptian warriors. It was not nearly as common as the spear or war club.

Nile Spear

The spear is one of the oldest weapons ever. The Egyptians would have used them extensively in their armies. It was the weapon of the rank and file, or common soldier. It had a sharp bronze head with a long wooden shaft. It was most effective with an Egyptian shield.

Javelin

The javelin is simply a slightly smaller spear used as a missile weapon. Ancient people used it for hunting as well as war. In the case of war, it would probably have a copper or bronze head. It could be thrown a good distance and was quite accurate in a skilled hand.

War Club

The club is another very ancient weapon used by many cultures. It is depicted in the earliest forms of Egyptian art work. The Egyptians used it extensively in the Bronze Age. Its heavy metal head could inflict serious wounds when used by a competent warrior.

New Kingdom Bronze Axe

The axe was used as a farming implement as well as a weapon of war. It was made with a wooden shaft and a head of bronze and used exclusively for chopping at the enemy. This type of axe remained in use by Egyptian soldiers well into the Iron Age, long after other bronze weapons were obsolete.

Crescent Axe

Another type of Bronze Age axe, this axe was used by the Egyptians as well as the Phoenicians and Carthaginians. Its long, curved blade was a very effective cutting instrument and was used fairly often by Egyptian warriors although not as much as the New Kingdom Bronze Axe. It is also depicted on early Egyptian art work.

Khopesh

The khopesh was a signature Egyptian weapon, although it was probably invented by the Canaanites. This bronze sword had an unusual, deep curve which helped prevent it from bending or breaking while in battle. Its main purpose was for cutting and chopping but later improvements allowed it to be effective in thrusting, hooking and punching one's enemies. The khopesh was truly a terrifying weapon on the battle field.

At first, there were 2 kinds of khopesh. The first one had a sharp hook-like point on the tip of the blade which was used for snaring the enemy by the armor or tunic. The second khopesh had no hook but was simply a curved blade, better for stabbing. Both types had pros and cons and eventually they were combined into one model, which is now the khopesh we recognize today.

Description of the Battle Game

Battling is at least two teams fighting each other using weapons. We suggest using our foam weapons to minimize injuries.

Divide your players into two teams of about the same strength and even numbers. Say there are four big guys and four little guys. There should be two big guys and two little guys on each team.

Weather is no deterrent to battling. We have had battles in rain and heat.

Object of the game: divide and conquer your enemy!

More than one battle can be played. It is important to keep score of who wins each battle. The one who wins the most battles is the victor!

You can use fortifications. Tree houses work well. Piles of logs or even swing sets can be used.

Naval battles can be fought using non-motor boats such as canoes and row boats. To fight a naval battle, simply row up to them and fight them. Do not use throwing axes, they are not waterproof.

With fortifications, it is often wise to use your spear instead of your axe or sword. The spear has greater length which is helpful in forts. It is very wise to use missiles (water balloons, throwing axes, etc.) so you can bombard the enemy without having to storm the gate.

It is crucial to use shields. People who do not use shields are usually slain early in the battle and are vulnerable to throwing axes and heavy weapons such as battle axes.

Terrible war cries intimidate the enemy.

It is important to have one main leader (general). This keeps the army unified and reduces squabbles.

Rules of the Battle Game

Rule #1

Chivalry and honor must be exhibited at all times.

Rule #2

If any weapon hits your limb (for ex. arm, leg, hand), you are no longer able to use it.
If you are holding a weapon in the hand or arm that is hit, you can't keep using the weapon with that arm but could switch it to the other arm and keep fighting. If both arms are hit, you must surrender or run away.

If your leg is hit, you must limp. If both legs are hit, you must kneel or squat. If you lose all your limbs, you are doomed!

Rule #3

If you get hit in the head, neck or torso, you are officially dead and can't play until the end of the battle.

Rule #4

The only way to win a battle is when all of the enemy (other team) are dead, have surrendered or have run away (escaped).
If a team holding prisoners is defeated, the prisoners are automatically freed.

Rule #5

If someone surrenders, you can either keep them captive, (they are not allowed to escape) or release them and they are free to return to their army (team).

Rule #6

Parley~ a parley is when one or possibly two people from each team talk to each other. To start a parley, one team member must say, "Request an audience". If the other team agrees, they send a person forward to talk to the other.
It is usually used for discussing the release of prisoners by ransom or switching of players. You can be chivalrous and release prisoners. It is important to not carry weapons but must leave them behind during a parley to avoid treachery.

Rule #7

We believe that only boys should battle with other boys. Young men should practice protecting young ladies so it is not appropriate to fight them.

Rule #8

Ransom~A ransom is when a soldier who is captured is released by a payment of money. You can make your own money (see instructions). To ransom a prisoner, first call a parley and then negotiate the price. A general usually costs more than the average soldier. (This rule is optional.)

Weapon Instructions

Introduction:

PVC pipe tips: You can find PVC pipe at your local hardware store like Lowe's and Home Depot. You will need a pipe cutter or a saw to cut the PVC pipe to the correct length. If you do not have a saw, the large hardware stores will usually cut it for you.

PVC pipe insulation~the black foam stuff. We usually buy this at the same stores as the PVC pipe. We like the kind that comes in a 4 pack of 3 foot pieces. It says on the package that it is for copper pipe but it works just fine for these weapons.

Foam~the 2 inch thick green stuff. You can find this foam at Wal-Mart and fabric stores like JoAnn.com and Hobby Lobby. It comes in small packages or in large pieces by the yard.

Cardboard: It can be difficult to cut cardboard so younger kids might need some help or supervision. In most of the pieces that use cardboard, it is important to cut the cardboard so the "ridges" (inner corrugated sections) **run across** the narrow width of the piece. This way the piece can bend properly. Check instructions before tracing the pattern onto the cardboard.

½ Width Piece of Duct Tape: Before we begin the weapon instructions, we need to define a term we will use in the book: "½ width". To make a ½ width piece of duct tape, take a piece of duct tape and tear it lengthwise (the long way). Now you have two ½ width pieces of duct tape. Sometimes, even a ¼ width piece of duct tape is used. Just tear the ½ width piece again to make the ¼ width.

Now, on to the fun!

Short Sword

Materials:

22 inch piece of ¾ inch PVC pipe
19 inch piece of PVC pipe insulation
(We use 3/8" thick polyethylene foam, fits ¾" pipe)
1 piece of foam 4" by 2" by 2" thick
Pattern
Marker
Duct tape
Scissors
(You may need a saw to cut the PVC to size)
        Please Note: This project may require adult help to use the sharp tools.

Directions:

Print and cut out the pattern for the pommel (p. 48). Lay the pattern on the foam, trace the pommel on the foam using a permanent marker and then cut it out. Then cut it in half so the piece is 1 inch thick.

Next, take the piece of black insulation and slide it down the PVC pipe.

6

Leave about 1 inch extending off of the PVC at the point of the sword and about 4 inches of the PVC pipe exposed.

Using a long piece, duct tape around the insulation where the blade meets the handle and pinch to the PVC.

Take a ½ width piece of duct tape (see page 5 for instructions on ½ width tape) and tape around the pinched area to secure it to the PVC pipe.

Wrap a piece of duct tape over the end of the sword. Press down the edges. Turn and repeat, making sure the edges are neatly pressed down. Wrap a piece of duct tape around the end for a smooth finish.

On the opposite end of the sword, apply the pommel to the bottom of the grip.

Place the piece of foam into the PVC pipe.

Using ½ width pieces of duct tape, tape the pommel onto the pipe. First, tape straight from one side of the pipe, over the pommel to the other side of the pipe. Be sure the strips aren't too tight on the pommel piece. It could cause the pommel to be crooked.

 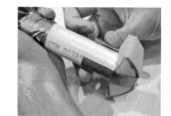

Tape again on a slight angle around the pommel to reinforce it.

To strengthen the pommel, tape on a sideways angle around the foam again as shown. Do this on both sides.

Keep the shape of the foam by not pressing too hard.

Now tape the flat edge of the pommel. Place a piece of duct tape on the flat edge and smooth around the pommel on a slight angle. Do this on the other side.

 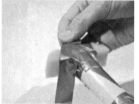  

Continue working around the pommel, adding more tape.

Now for the tip, again place the piece of tape on the flat side, carefully wrap around the tip. Then, place a piece up and over the tip of the pommel.

 Cover the grip with duct tape.

Now tape the blade. It is helpful to have another person. Start at the hilt and wrap on a slightly diagonal angle towards the tip of the blade.

Cover any open spots with more duct tape.

The interesting thing about early Egyptian swords is that they had a substantial mound in the center of their grip. It was much different than the swords of Medieval Europe. The thicker handle worked very well for a one-handed sword instead of a two-handed sword. This allowed the warrior to have a stronger, more powerful, grip on the weapon.

Just use a lot of tape on the grip (handle). Start with a full size piece of duct tape. As you wrap around the grip, use strips that are narrower.

To get a more rounded feel, tape over the edges of the mound of tape on angles, going around several times.

Decorate as desired.

You're done!

Nile Spear

Materials:

60 inch (5 foot) piece of ¾ inch PVC pipe
  (It could be shorter for a smaller child)
14 inch piece of PVC pipe insulation
  (We use 3/8" thick polyethylene foam, fits ¾" pipe)
1 piece of foam 12" by 6" by 2" thick
Patterns
Marker
Scissors
Duct tape
(You may need a saw or pipe cutter to cut the PVC to size)
Please Note: This project may require adult help to use the sharp tools

Directions:

Print and cut out the pattern for the spear (p. 49). Lay the pattern on the foam, trace around the pattern using a permanent marker. Flip the pattern over and trace again. Cut them out.

Next, take the piece of insulation and slide it down the PVC pipe.

Leave about 2 inches extending off of the PVC pipe at the point of the spear.

Using a long piece, duct tape around the insulation where the spear tip meets the handle and pinch to the PVC. Take a ½ width piece of duct tape (see page 5 for instructions on ½ width tape) and tape around the pinched area to secure it to the PVC pipe.

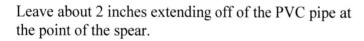

Wrap a piece of duct tape over the end of the spear tip. Press down the edges. Turn and repeat, making sure the edges are neatly pressed down. Wrap a piece of duct tape around the end for a smooth finish.

Cover the end of the PVC pipe. Take a square piece of duct tape and put it on the end of the pipe. Press the edges down around the PVC pipe. Wrap another piece of tape around the end to give a smooth finish. Usually, we use a ½ width piece of duct tape.

Add more duct tape around the top and bottom of the spear tip to reinforce it.

Place a green foam piece next to the spear tip in the center, about 3 inches from the end.
Tape over the lower end, being careful to keep the shape of the foam.
Wrap the duct tape all the way around the black insulation part.

Tape over the tip of the foam and keep adding tape going down the foam piece.

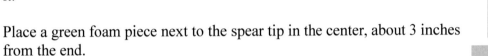

Using a ½ width piece of duct tape, tape the lower end of the foam diagonally from the spear tip around the foam and back onto the spear tip.

Wrap a ½ width piece of duct tape around the spear tip to reinforce the diagonal piece.

Continue to cover the inner curve of the green foam with pieces of duct tape. Be careful to keep the shape of the foam as you tape.

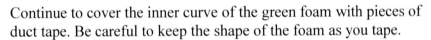

Wrap a piece of duct tape over the end of the foam.

Now place a piece of duct tape down and around the end of the foam. Use small pieces to cover any foam that is showing on the edges.

Lay the second piece of green foam next to the spear tip, making sure it lines up with the first piece. Basically, repeat the steps for taping the foam onto the spear tip.

Tape over the tip of the foam. Tape over the lower end, being careful to keep the shape of the foam. Wrap the duct tape all the way around the black insulation part. Keep adding tape going down the foam piece.

Using a ½ width piece of duct tape, tape the lower end of the foam diagonally from the spear tip around the foam and back onto the spear tip. Wrap a ½ width piece of duct tape around the spear tip to reinforce the diagonal piece

Continue to cover the inner curve of the green foam with pieces of duct tape. Be careful to keep the shape of the foam as you tape.

Now place a piece of duct tape down and around the end of the foam. Use small pieces to cover any foam that is showing on the edges.

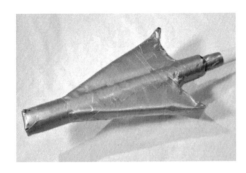

Cover the handle of the Nile spear with any color you choose. You can use a long strip or wrap duct tape around the handle.

Decorate as desired.

Javelin

Materials:

5 inch piece of ¾ inch PVC pipe
2 feet 7 inch piece of PVC pipe insulation (we'll call it foam)
Duct tape
Scissors
(You may need a pipe cutter or saw to cut the PVC to size)
        Please Note: This project may require adult help to use the sharp tools.

Directions:

Slide the PVC pipe into the foam until it is about 3 inches **in** from the end. (It is the weight to keep the javelin flying straight.)

It should not be visible past the foam.

Wrap a piece of duct tape over the end of the javelin. Press down the edges. Turn and repeat, making sure the edges are neatly pressed down. Wrap a piece of duct tape around the end for a smooth finish. Tape around the foam a couple of times where the piece of PVC pipe is to keep the foam from splitting.

To make the frill, cut a piece of duct tape 6 inches long. Place on foam long-ways but only press down half of the width of the tape.

Lay the next piece about 1 inch from the first piece. Press onto the foam and then pinch together with the first piece so that it stands up.

Do this 2 more times to make 3 frills. Position the duct tape so that the frills are on 3 opposite sides, like N, SE and SW on the compass, as shown below.

Trim the top of the frills on the diagonal.

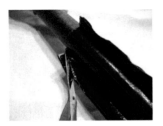

This javelin is pretty safe and we use it in battling. But use it at your own risk.

War Club

Materials:

24 inch piece of ¾ inch PVC pipe
8 inch piece of PVC pipe insulation
(We use 3/8" thick polyethylene foam, fits ¾" pipe)
Scrap pieces of 2" thick foam or about 12" x 12"
Marker
Duct tape
Scissors
(You may need a saw to cut the PVC to size)
Please Note: This project may require adult help to use the sharp tools.

Directions:

Take the black piece of insulation and slide it down the PVC pipe. Make the end of the black insulation even with the end of the PVC pipe.

Using a long piece, duct tape around the insulation where the black insulation meets the handle and pinch to the PVC. Take a ½ width piece of duct tape (see page 5 for instructions on ½ width tape) and tape around the pinched area to secure it to the PVC pipe.

Wrap a piece of duct tape over the end of the war club. Press down the edges. Turn and repeat, making sure the edges are neatly pressed down. Wrap a piece of duct tape around the end for a smooth finish.

Cut a small circle of green foam about 4 or 5 inches across. Sculpt a dome shape out of the circle of foam by cutting off small pieces until you get the look you want.

There is no special way to make the head of the war club. Basically, tape on pieces of foam around the end to form a rounded oval shape. Use the scraps of foam and fit them around the black insulation completely covering it.

Cover the main part of the war club head with duct tape.

Tape the dome shaped piece of foam (that you cut earlier) onto the top of the war club. Cover it in duct tape.

   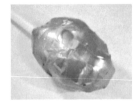

Using a small piece of foam about 3 inches long and about an inch wide, trim the sides to form a spike.

Cover the spike in duct tape. Carefully tape around the foam, making sure to keep the shape of the foam.

Place the spike on the top of the war club. Using ½ width pieces of duct tape, tape the spike firmly to the club. Place the tape on the spike and press down onto the war club. Be sure the spike is straight as you tape.

Now, tape around the base of the spike to secure it.

Cover the end of the PVC pipe. Take a square piece of duct tape and put it on the end of the pipe. Press the edges down around the PVC pipe. Wrap another piece of tape around the end to give a smooth finish. Usually, we use a ½ width piece of duct tape.

Cover the handle of the war club with any color you choose. You can use a long strip or wrap duct tape around the handle.

Decorate the war club as you like. Good job!

New Kingdom Bronze Axe

Materials:
30 inch piece of ¾ inch PVC pipe
6 inch piece of PVC pipe insulation
(We use 3/8" thick polyethylene foam, fits ¾" pipe)
1 piece of foam 9" by 7" by 2" thick and (1) 5" by 3" by 2"
Patterns
Marker
Duct tape
Scissors
(You may need a saw to cut the PVC to size)
> Please Note: This project may require adult help to use the sharp tools.

Directions:
Print and cut out the patterns for the axe. You will need the blade and handle pieces (p. 50, 51). Lay the patterns on the foam, trace around the patterns on the foam using a permanent marker and then cut them out.

Next, take the piece of insulation and slide it down the PVC pipe.

Leave about 1 inch extending off of the PVC at the point of the axe.

Using a long piece, duct tape around the insulation where the axe head meets the handle and pinch to the PVC. Take a ½ width piece of duct tape (see page 5 for instructions on ½ width tape) and tape around the pinched area to secure it to the PVC pipe.

Wrap a piece of duct tape over the end of the axe. Press down the edges. Turn and repeat, making sure the edges are neatly pressed down. Wrap a piece of duct tape around the end for a smooth finish.

Place the green foam against the tip of the axe next to the black insulation. Carefully tape the top of the axe head with a piece of duct tape placed at an angle. Have the duct tape reach all the way around.

Repeat for the bottom edge of the blade. Reinforce with another piece of tape and cover the green foam.

At the bottom part of the axe head, place another piece of duct tape. Make sure the duct tape is long enough to reach around to the pipe insulation. Do the same on the top of the axe head.

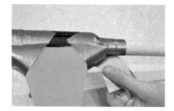   

As you can see from the pictures, we wrapped the top and bottom of the axe head on an angle 3 times on each end. Be careful to keep the shape of the foam when wrapping the duct tape.

Using a long piece of duct tape, start taping around the thinner, middle section of the axe head.

Keep taping out toward the edge of the blade. Try to retain the shape of the foam as you tape.

Use a long piece of duct tape and tape around the edge of the blade. Take shorter pieces of duct tape and tape over the sides.

   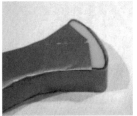

For the end, wrap tape around the edge of the axe head to cover all of the green foam.

  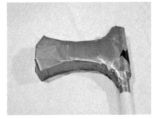

Cover any foam that shows on the back of the axe head with more duct tape.

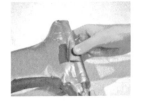 

Cover the end of the PVC pipe. Place a piece of duct tape over the end. Press the edges down around the PVC pipe. Wrap another piece of tape around the end to give a smooth finish.

The end of the axe is called the swell knob. To make the swell knob, place the foam piece cut from the swell knob pattern next to the end of the PVC pipe.

BE SURE the swell knob piece lines up with the axe blade. (See picture)

Tape the top of the triangle to the PVC pipe.

Tape the larger end of the triangle to the PVC pipe. Be careful that it is straight.

Place duct tape in the middle, covering all of the green foam.

Then tape the very bottom of the swell knob. Wrap carefully to keep the shape of the foam. Press in the edges of the duct tape near the PVC pipe. Cover any bits of green foam that may be showing with small pieces of tape.

Reinforce the top of the swell knob for strength. Cover the shaft of the axe with any color you like. Wrap the tape around on an angle to cover smoothly.

Decorate the axe as you desire.

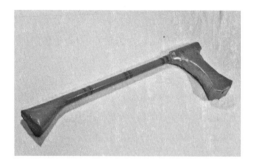 

Crescent Axe

Materials:
28 inch piece of ¾ inch PVC pipe
15 inch piece of PVC pipe insulation
(We use 3/8" thick polyethylene foam, fits ¾" pipe)
1 piece of foam 14" by 6" by 2" thick
Pattern
Marker
Duct tape
Scissors
(You may need a saw to cut the PVC to size)
  Please Note: This project may require adult help to use the sharp tools.

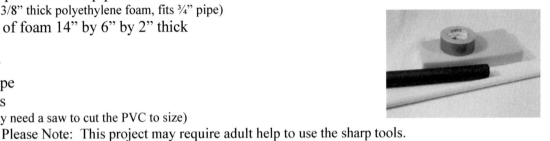

Directions:
Print and cut out the patterns for the crescent axe (p. 52, 53). Tape the pattern pieces together. Lay the pattern on the foam, trace around the pattern on the foam using a permanent marker and then cut it out.

Next, take the piece of pipe insulation and slide it down the PVC pipe.

Leave about 1 inch extending off of the PVC at the point of the axe.

Using a long piece of duct tape, tape around the insulation where the axe head meets the handle and pinch to the PVC.

Take a ½ width piece of duct tape (see page 5 for instructions on ½ width tape) and tape around the pinched area to secure it to the PVC pipe.

Wrap a piece of duct tape over the end of the axe. Press down the edges. Turn and repeat, making sure the edges are neatly pressed down. Wrap a piece of duct tape around the end for a smooth finish.

Tape the inside of the curve of the axe blade. Place a piece of duct tape on the inside of the curve of the green foam near the center part. Carefully wrap the tape around the foam. Try to retain the shape of the foam as you tape. Place another piece of tape on the other side of the center part.

 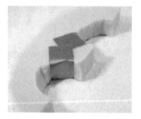  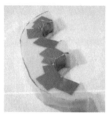

Carefully work around the curves. Continue until the inner curves are covered in duct tape.

Place the green foam next to the top of the axe by the black insulation (the shaft of the axe). Line up the green foam with the top of the axe.

Using a long piece of duct tape, wrap the tape from the foam, around the pipe and over the center part of the green foam. Now tape the top and bottom parts of the green foam.

Starting in the center part of the foam, tape diagonally from the shaft through the opening and over the shaft again for extra strength. Be sure to catch the edge of the foam with the tape. Now, tape around the base of the center part of the green foam to strengthen it.

 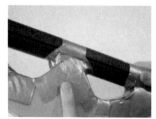 

24

Tape around the shaft inside the curved sections near the center foam section, covering the diagonal piece of duct tape.

To secure the bottom and top sections of the crescent axe, tape diagonally inside the curved areas of foam.

 Put a piece of tape over the diagonal piece of duct tape around the shaft to continue to secure it.

At the bottom of the axe head, tape around the end to the shaft. Also at the top of the axe head, tape across the shaft and green foam to secure it.

Cover all of the black insulation on the shaft with duct tape.

Cover the axe blade (green foam) with duct tape. Tape from the side over the edge of the blade and back around to the side. Be careful to maintain the shape of the foam.

Make sure the duct tape is evenly spaced. Don't overlap it too much or it makes the weapon too heavy. Cover up any remaining foam that shows through.

Cover the end of the PVC pipe. Place a piece of duct tape over the end. Press the edges down around the PVC pipe.

Wrap another piece of tape around the end to give a smooth finish.

Cover the handle of the crescent axe with any color you choose. You can use a long strip or wrap duct tape around the handle.

Decorate as desired.

Khopesh

Materials:

13 inch piece of ¾ inch PVC pipe
7.5 inch piece of black PVC pipe insulation
(We use 3/8" thick polyethylene foam, fits ¾" pipe)
1 piece of foam 23" by 8" by 2" thick and another piece 4" x 2"
Patterns
Cardboard
Marker
Duct tape
Scissors
Clear "scotch" tape
(You may need a saw to cut the PVC to size)
> Please Note: This project may require adult help to use the sharp tools.

Directions:

Print and cut out the patterns for the khopesh. You need the khophesh blade lower piece and upper piece patterns, khopesh spiked pommel pattern and the khopesh stabilizer pattern (p. 54-57). The blade upper and lower pieces need to be taped together at the edge of the paper to complete the pattern.

Lay the blade and spiked pommel patterns on the foam, trace around the patterns on the foam using a permanent marker and then cut them out. (Sorry, no picture.)

Trace the khopesh stabilizer piece onto the cardboard 2 times and cut out.

Next, take the piece of black insulation and slide it down the PVC pipe. Make the end of the black insulation even with the end of the PVC pipe.

Using a long piece, duct tape around the insulation where the black insulation meets the handle and pinch to the PVC. Take a ½ width piece of duct tape (see page 5 for instructions on ½ width tape) and tape around the pinched area to secure it to the PVC pipe.

Wrap a piece of duct tape over the end of the khopesh. Press down the edges. Turn and repeat, making sure the edges are neatly pressed down. Wrap a piece of duct tape around the end for a smooth finish.

Lay the foam blade piece and the handle on a flat surface so that they are properly aligned. You may need a helper to help you tape the first part of the khopesh.

Have the helper hold the handle in one hand and the foam blade piece resting on the top of the handle. Wrap a piece of duct tape around the foam stem and all the way around the upper handle. Tape around this section several times.

Tape from the stem up and on to the curve of the blade.

The sharp part of the blade would have been on the outer curve of the blade.

At the lower edge of the blade is a hook. Tape under the hook and then again around the front of the handle near the hook. As you tape the foam, be careful to keep the shape of the foam by not taping too tightly.

Using a ½ width piece of duct tape, tape underneath the hook and around the sides of the blade. Tape again for strength.

Begin to tape the blade. Alternate wrapping the duct tape around the front and back of the blade. Wrap a few times.

Once there are a couple strips of tape around the blade, lay the khopesh stabilizer piece on the side of the blade. Tape around the stabilizer and blade at least 2 times.

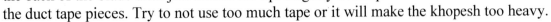

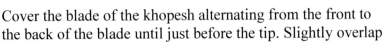

Then do the same to the other side of the khopesh. Carefully cover the stabilizer with more duct tape, being careful to maintain the shape of the foam.

Cover the blade of the khopesh alternating from the front to the back of the blade until just before the tip. Slightly overlap the duct tape pieces. Try to not use too much tape or it will make the khopesh too heavy.

To tape the tip of the khopesh, use ½ width pieces of duct tape and carefully tape under the tip. When you get to the edge, tape over the top.

Starting on the side of the tip, wrap a piece of duct tape up and over the edge. Continue to cover the tip with whatever size pieces fit the best.

Egyptian weapons would have had a thicker grip on the handle. To cover the handle of the khopesh, use a lot of tape to create a thicker area. Start with a full size piece of duct tape. As you wrap around the handle, use strips that are narrower. To get a more rounded feel on the handle, tape over the edges of the mound of tape on an angle, going around several times.

Spiked pommel

Cut the spiked pommel piece of foam in half so it is only 1 inch thick.

Cover in duct tape first. The flat side of the spiked pommel will be against the handle so it doesn't need to be covered in duct tape. Using narrow strips of duct tape, tape the inside curve.

Carefully tape around the tip of the spiked pommel keeping the shape of the foam.

Lay the khopesh flat and line up the spiked pommel piece just at the bottom of the handle. See the picture for details. Wrap a piece of duct tape around the lower end of the pommel.

Continue to tape going up the pommel securing it to the handle. Wrap a final full piece of duct tape around the handle and the spiked pommel to reinforce it.

Decorate as you like. Great job!

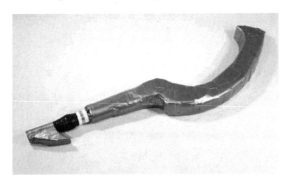 

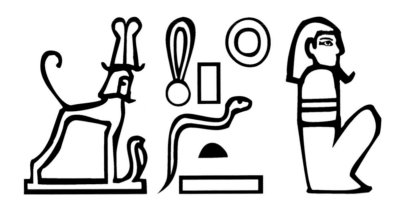

Pharaoh's Belt

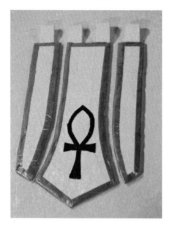

Materials:
Cardboard piece of at least 14 inches by 8 inches
Patterns
Marker
Duct tape
Scissors
Belt (the belt does not become a permanent part of the armor)

Directions:
Print patterns for the Pharaoh's belt (p. 58-60). The bottom point of the Pharaoh's belt should be right above the knee. Measure the distance from the waist (or where a belt would go) to just above the knee. The main pattern piece should be about this long. You may need to lengthen the patterns. Add length on the top of the patterns so the piece is long enough for the person wearing the Pharaoh's belt. The top of the pattern is right at the belt area (waist).
Trace the patterns onto cardboard and cut out.

Cover all the pieces of cardboard with duct tape. It's best to cover the edges first so they are smooth.

Add decoration to the belt piece. I usually trace out a design first and then add tape. This is the hieroglyph that represents "life". It was often worn by Pharaohs.

Rip thin pieces of duct tape and place in the design.

I added gold trim around the edge to give it a more decorative feel. Gold was a popular metal in Egypt that was commonly worn by royalty. Use a ½ width piece of duct tape (See p.5) and wrap around the edge (but not the very top edge).

Make 4 duct tape loops. For 1 loop, use a piece of duct tape 5 inches long by 1 inch wide. (Tear the duct tape piece in half.) Put a shorter piece of tape that is 4 inches by 1 inch inside on the sticky part of the 5 inch piece. That leaves a ½ inch of the sticky part hanging out on both ends.

Place the sticky part of the loop on the back corner of the top of the center belt piece. Bend the loop over and press the sticky ½ inch part on the front of the belt piece. Put another loop on the other top corner.

Now add some more ½ width pieces of gold duct tape over the edge at the top and a ¼ width piece of gold duct tape at the very top edge.

Add a ½ width piece of white duct tape to the top of the **back** of the belt piece to strengthen the loops.

Trim the side pieces of the belt in gold duct tape also, using a ½ width piece of tape, except for the top edge. That will come later. Place the loop at the center of the top on the back, bend it over and press the sticky part onto the front of the belt piece.

Finish the gold trim near the loop. Using a ¼ width piece of gold duct tape, finish the top of the side belt piece. Do this for both side pieces.

Add a ½ width piece of white duct tape to the top of the **back** of the side belt pieces to strengthen the loops. Add another white piece on the front of the side belt piece.

Slide the loops onto a belt and put around the waist. You're done!

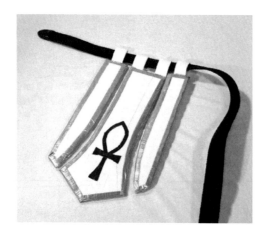 

Neck Armor

Materials:
Cardboard piece of at least 17 inches by 13 inches and
another piece 5 inches by 5 inches
Patterns
Marker
Duct tape
Scissors
Elastic about 48 inches long, about ¾" wide (see instructions)
Stapler/Staples

Directions:

Print the patterns for the neck armor and cut them out (p. 61, 62). You need the neck armor piece
and the shoulder extension piece. The neck armor pattern needs to be printed 2 times and taped
together at the edge of the paper to complete the pattern. Trace the patterns onto cardboard and
cut out them out.

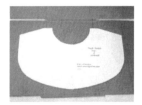   

Cover the inside neck edge of the main neck armor piece with duct
tape. We use ½ width pieces of duct tape because it gives a smoother
finish. (See instructions for ½ width tape strips on page 5.) Cover all
the side and lower edges of the main neck armor piece.

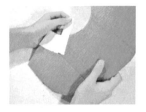

Completely cover the front with white duct tape or a color of your
choice. We cover the back, too.

Now for the shoulder extensions, fold a piece of duct tape over the edge for a clean look. Completely cover with duct tape.

Line up the shoulder extensions near the side edge of the main piece and about ¼ inch above. (See picture) Tape the shoulder extensions to the main piece on the front and back sides. Keep the ¼ inch gap.

Try on the neck armor and measure how long the elastic needs to be. The elastic should start at the shoulder extension, cross the back and attach under the arm at the lower edge of the main piece about 6 inches down from the corner of the main piece. Our piece of elastic was 24 inches.

Staple the elastic to the armor pieces with the staples going through to the front. (The picture shows the back of the armor.)

First, staple the end of the elastic to the shoulder extension. Have the end of the elastic facing into the armor so it looks better.

 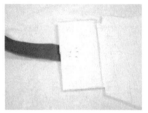

Then, staple the end of the elastic to the side of the neck armor. We placed the elastic about 6 inches down from the corner. Cover all staples with duct tape on the front and back of the armor.

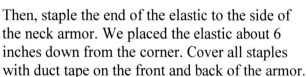

Now, repeat with the other strap of elastic, crossing over the first piece of elastic.

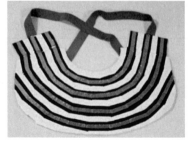

Decorate as you like.   Great job!

Wrist Armor

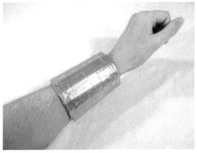

Materials:

Cardboard pieces (2) of at least 7 inches by 8 inches
   Or whatever fits the wrist of the wearer
Marker
Duct tape, gold or gray
Scissors
Elastic about 6 inches long, about ¾" wide
Stapler/Staples

Directions:

Egyptian pharaohs and foot soldiers often wore arm bands. The arm bands were protective and decorative. People of greater importance would wear more valuable metals.

Measure around the wrist and add 1 inch. Measure around the middle of the forearm and add 1 inch. Now measure the length from the wrist to the middle of the forearm, or how long you want the wrist armor pieces to be. This is the size of your wrist armor.

Center the wrist measurement over the forearm measurement so it forms a trapezoid.

Please note: For the cardboard pieces, be sure to cut the cardboard so the "ridges" (inner corrugated sections) **run across** the narrow width of the piece. This way the piece can bend properly.

Cut out the 2 pieces. Curve the cardboard.

Completely cover the inside with long strips so ends of the duct tape don't rub against the skin.

Cover the outside with duct tape.

Cut 2 pieces of elastic 3 inches long. Position them on the inside of the wrist armor. Staple toward the outside so the points of the staples are not near the skin.

Cover the staples with duct tape inside and outside.

Try on the wrist armor and mark where the other ends of the elastic should go, usually about 1 inch will be inside the edge.

Staple the elastic ends with a few staples. Cover the staples on both sides with duct tape.

Make another one just like it! Now you have a complete set of wrist armor!

Nemes~Egyptian Head gear

Pharaoh and Foot Soldier

Materials:

Cardboard piece, 1 inch wide by the length around the head plus 2 inches and another piece 4" x 3"
Marker, pencil
Duct tape, gold or gray
White large men's t-shirt (or a piece of white fabric 48" x 19")
Scissors
Ruler or measuring tape
Clear "scotch" tape
Stapler/Staples
Optional: sewing pins or safety pins

Directions:

These are the directions for the pharaoh nemes. Measure the distance around the head, the circumference. Cut a piece of cardboard this length plus 2 inches and 1 inch wide. Print the pattern for the nemes cobra ornament (p. 63). Trace the pattern onto the cardboard and cut out. There are 2 pieces in the ornament pattern.

Cover both sides of the cardboard strip in gold duct tape. Find the center of the strip and put a mark on the inside. Place the cardboard strip up against the head of the person who is going to wear it. Make a little mark on the strip right behind the ears. There should be 3 marks on the inside of the strip.
(The pictures are in gray but you get the idea.)

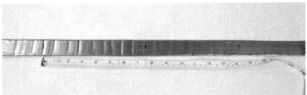

Lay the t-shirt out flat and cut smoothly down the center of the front. (Don't cut the back.) If you are using fabric, skip this step. ☺

Hold the hem at the bottom of the shirt; find the center of the back. Place this center spot on the center mark on the cardboard strip. Spread out the hem of the shirt, without stretching, to the other 2 marks. Hold the shirt (fabric) down with scotch tape if that helps. Yes, the hem is on the strip.
If you are using fabric, find the center of the 48 inches and place on the center mark on the strip.

Carefully staple the shirt (fabric) to the strip ONLY just inside the 2 outside marks. Use plenty of staples close together.

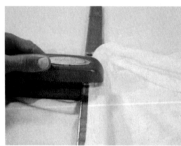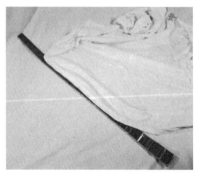

Cover the outside of the strip with a ½ width piece of duct tape to cover the staple points. Do it again so they won't poke through. (See instructions for ½ width duct tape strips on page 5.)

Now try on the nemes. I suggest tipping the head over. Place the strip on the forehead and fold over the ends of the strip. Put a little mark where they meet or hold it tightly. Wrap the ends with duct tape to secure them.

Put the nemes on (again with the head tipped over) then lift head and flip the white fabric back. The white fabric should tuck behind the ears and have a nice fold on the top. (See picture.)

Now to trim the shirt. The nemes should reach just to the shoulders, or a little over, in the back. You could safely trim the white fabric to 19 inches and then mark where to cut the sides. That's what worked for us. Put it on the person who will wear it. Starting at the back of the head, pin (with sewing pins, safety pins) or mark with a pencil where you need to cut. But not all the way around.....

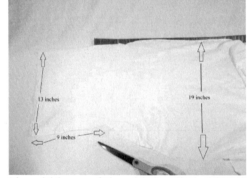

Work your way to the sides. Pull some fabric to the front so it hangs over the shoulder. Fold under the edge (the old hem of the shirt) a little bit. Pin so there is a strip hanging over the shoulder.

Lay flat and trim where you marked it. You'll end up trimming the front to look like the picture. Our measurements were 13 inches on the end, 9 inches in and a gentle curve around to the back. The other side is the same. Adjust to fit the wearer. Don't worry if it's not perfect. Try it on and trim as needed.

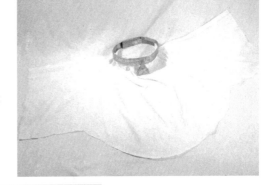

Now to add the cobra ornament:

Cover the larger ornament piece with gold duct tape. Place the small piece on a ½ width piece of gold duct tape. Carefully place it in the middle of the larger piece and press down.

Using a ½ width piece of gold duct tape, tape the cobra ornament to the center of the forehead strip. The emblem of the cobra was often used in Egyptian art particularly with royalty.

Directions for the foot soldier nemes:
The directions are the same except for a few little things. Use gray tape for the strip.

Cut the white t-shirt (fabric) into a gentle curve with no long strips. The common man wore the nemes to the shoulder. And, of course, it did not have an ornament.

Egyptian Shield

Materials:
Cardboard ~ whatever size you desire, we used 2 pieces of 27" x 30", plus another piece 13" x 5"
Duct Tape, white and gray
Scissors
Marker
Ruler
Stapler/Staples

Directions:
The Egyptian people used this type of shield for about 3700 years from their earliest battles under their pharaohs until well into the time of the Arabian occupation in 639 AD. They were often covered in leather.

Start with a large mostly square piece of cardboard and a good amount of duct tape. Create your shield size to fit the size of the person using it.

To make the top curve, measure the width of the piece of cardboard somewhat higher than the center. Find the middle point by dividing the number in half. Draw a dot at this point with the marker. To make a large compass, take a string, hold one end at the edge of the cardboard and the other end of the string on the dot. Hold a marker at the end of the string by the edge of the cardboard. With the marker at the end of the string, make a line in a curve for the top of the shield.

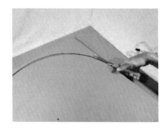

Cut along the curved line to create the top of the shield. It doesn't have to be perfect. This is duct tape, folks!

Make sure the grain of the corrugated cardboard for the 2 pieces is going in opposite directions. This strengthens the shield so it won't bend in the middle of the battle. Then trace the curve onto the second piece of cardboard. Cut it out.

Start by taping over the edges at the lower corners. This will keep the pieces together as you work. Continue to tape over the edge all the way around.

Cover the front of the shield with white duct tape, leaving a rim of gray duct tape around the edge. Use shorter pieces of white duct tape to keep the shape of the curved top.

The center circle on the outside of the shield is called a boss. Make a circle out of cardboard for the boss of the shield. We traced around a roll of duct tape and cut it out. It made a 6 inch circle.

Cover with gray duct tape, wrapping around the edge also.

Place a few pieces of gray duct tape hanging over the edge.

Measure the shield and mark the center of the width of the shield a little above the center.

Place the gray circle on the center mark, pressing down the tape pieces. Cover the gray duct tape outside the circle with pieces of white duct tape.

It's best to cover the back of the shield with gray duct tape. Otherwise the cardboard can chafe against the warrior's arm.

Please note: For the cardboard pieces, be sure to cut the cardboard so the "ridges" (inner corrugated sections) **run across** the narrow width of the piece. This way the piece can bend properly.

Cut a piece of cardboard 13 inches long by 2 inches wide. Cut another piece of cardboard 13 inches long by 3 inches wide. Leave one inch flat on each end and then crease the pieces so they have a nice curve.

Cover the cardboard strips with duct tape.

Place the strips on the back of the shield where you want them. We placed them on an angle because that is how real Egyptian shields were held. Feel free to adjust the strips so they are comfortable for you.

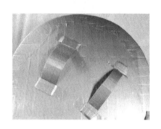

The wider 3 inch strip should go near the forearm. The narrow strip is for the hand grip. Use a small piece of tape to hold the strips in place while you try it out. Be sure to give your arm plenty of room. Adjust the strips as needed.

Staple the top ends of the strips to the shield many times. Cover the staples with duct tape. Staple the lower ends of the strips and tape over the ends to cover the staples and reinforce the strips.

Cover any staples that show through the front as needed.

Reinforce the ends by cross taping the duct tape again.

You're done!
Awesome!

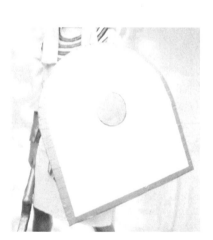

Tunic

Materials:
Some sort of fabric-knit, sheets, or whatever you have
Belt or material for a sash
Scissors
Sewing machine or needle and thread or duct tape!

Directions:
The tunic was the standard garb of Egypt, much like the jeans and t-shirt of today!
First determine the size you will need. The size of your fabric may determine the width or measure across the shoulders. Make it wide enough so that you can slip it over your head and shoulders and get the arms out of the arm holes. If you have enough fabric, double the length so you won't need to sew a seam across the shoulders.

Cut a hole for the head to go through. The No-Sew Option is to just pull the tunic over the head and use a belt to keep it around the waist, or put some duct tape down the sides to keep it together.

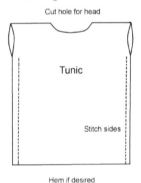

The sewing option is to sew up the sides but leave an arm hole. Hem the bottom if desired. Knit fabric is nice because it doesn't fray and you won't have to hem the edges.

If you want sleeves in your tunic, make a "T" shape of fabric and then sew up the sides. Be sure the main body of the tunic is wide enough so that you can get it on and get the arms through the sleeves.
Maybe almost double the width across the front (chest) of the person.

Some children are small and the hole in the neck will gap too much. Just add a button and loop at the back of the neck to close it a little, or a little piece of duct tape!

Use a belt or cut a strip of fabric to wrap around the waist.

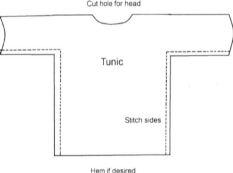

Money Pouch

Materials:

Fabric: see instructions
String, rope, ribbon, shoe lace or whatever you have
Safety pin
Scissors
Sewing machine or needle and thread
Option: Leg from a pair of cut off pants

Directions:

You can make a money pouch out of almost anything. If you want a money pouch that is a bit fancier, you can use fabric. We just happened to have a scrap of velour that we used for a pouch. Knit fabric won't fray and is easier but any durable fabric will work.

Determine the size of pouch that you want. For example, if you want a pouch that is 5" x 7", allowing for seam allowances and the casing for the drawstring, cut two (2) squares of 6" x 8 ½". You can also cut a long rectangle and just fold over so that you eliminate one seam. The rectangle would be 6" x 16".

Put the right sides together and sew up the seams leaving one 6" side open (use ½" seam). Turn over 1" at the opening. Stitch around using a small seam of about ¼". On the side or center front, make a small cut in the casing only on the front piece big enough for the drawstring to go through.

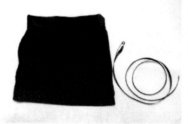 

Cut your drawstring to at least twice the length of your opening. In this example, the opening is 10" after sewing, so the drawstring should be 20" long. Put the safety pin in the end of the drawstring and push it through the casing.

A leg from a pair of pants that was cut off into shorts can be made into a pouch. Cut to the size you want. Sew one end. Cut small slits about an inch apart and weave your drawstring in and out through the slits. If you don't have any, thrift stores and yard sales often have pants for cheap.

Coin Money for Ransom

Materials:

Aluminum foil
Something heavy like a hammer or shoe

Directions:

Take a small piece of aluminum foil about twice the size you want the coin to be and fold in the edges to make a circle. It's all right if it is not perfectly round, ancient money wasn't perfect either. Press down firmly against a hard surface and then hammer flat with the heel of a shoe or a hammer.

Mark the coins with designs or figures so you know which coins belong to you. You can also make a money pouch to keep your money in while you are battling. See instructions for money pouch.

In Egypt, silver was more scarce than gold and possessed a higher value. The currency of Egypt was silver.

Short Sword Pommel
Cut 1
of
foam

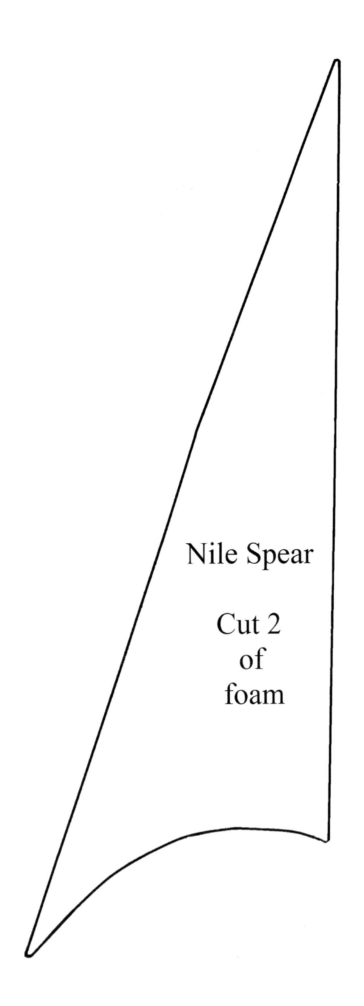

Nile Spear

Cut 2
of
foam

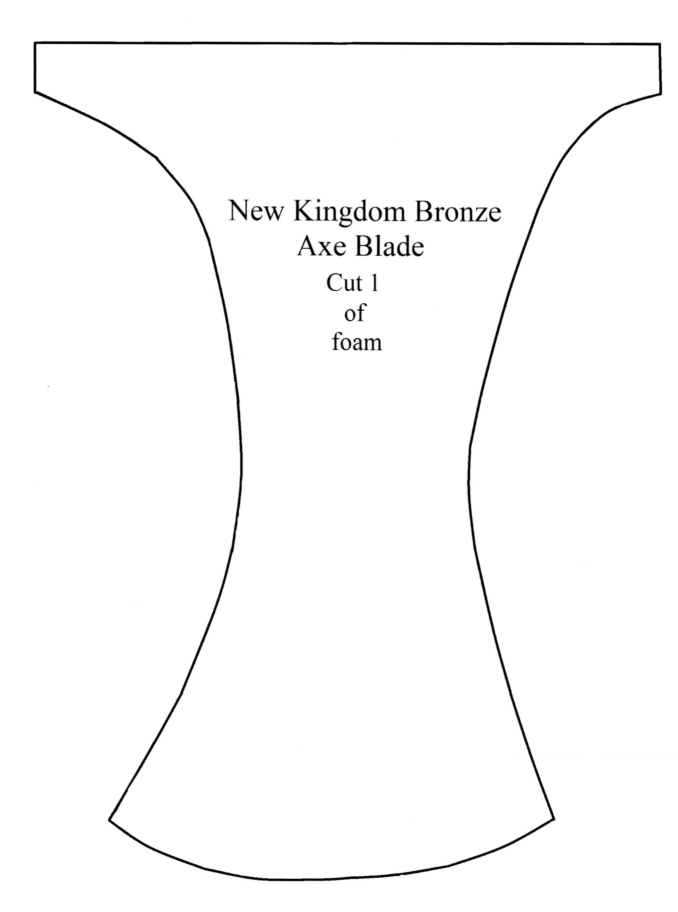

New Kingdom Bronze
Axe Blade
Cut 1
of
foam

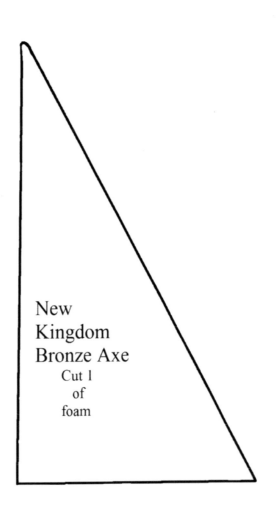

New
Kingdom
Bronze Axe
Cut 1
of
foam

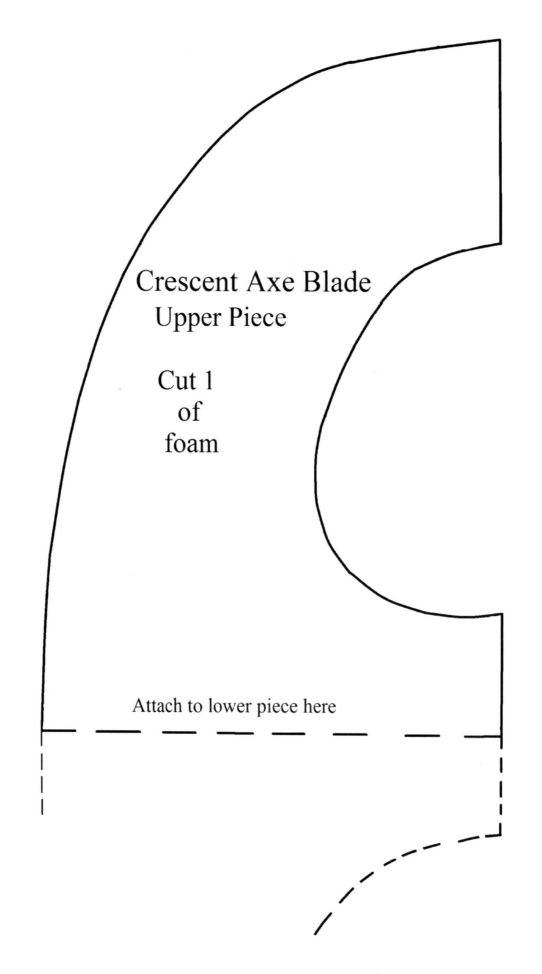

Crescent Axe Blade
Upper Piece

Cut 1
of
foam

Attach to lower piece here

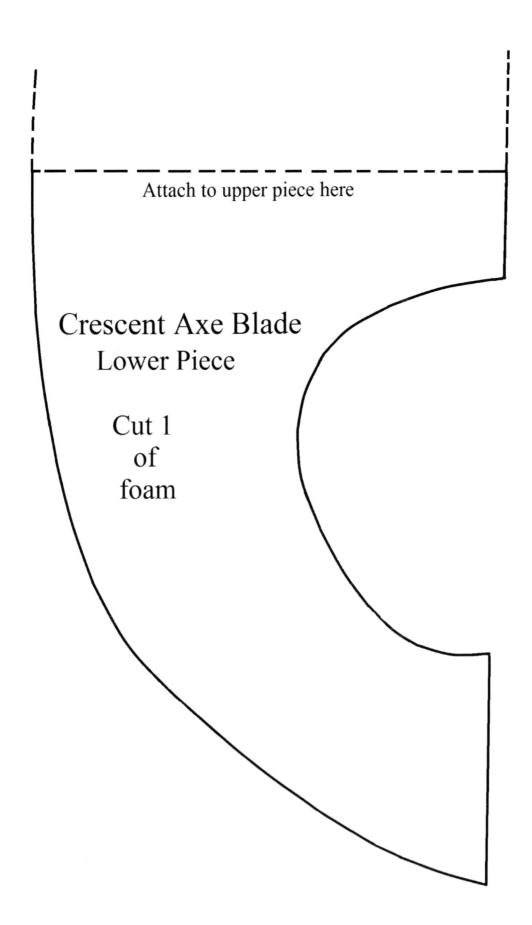

Attach to upper piece here

Crescent Axe Blade
Lower Piece

Cut 1
of
foam

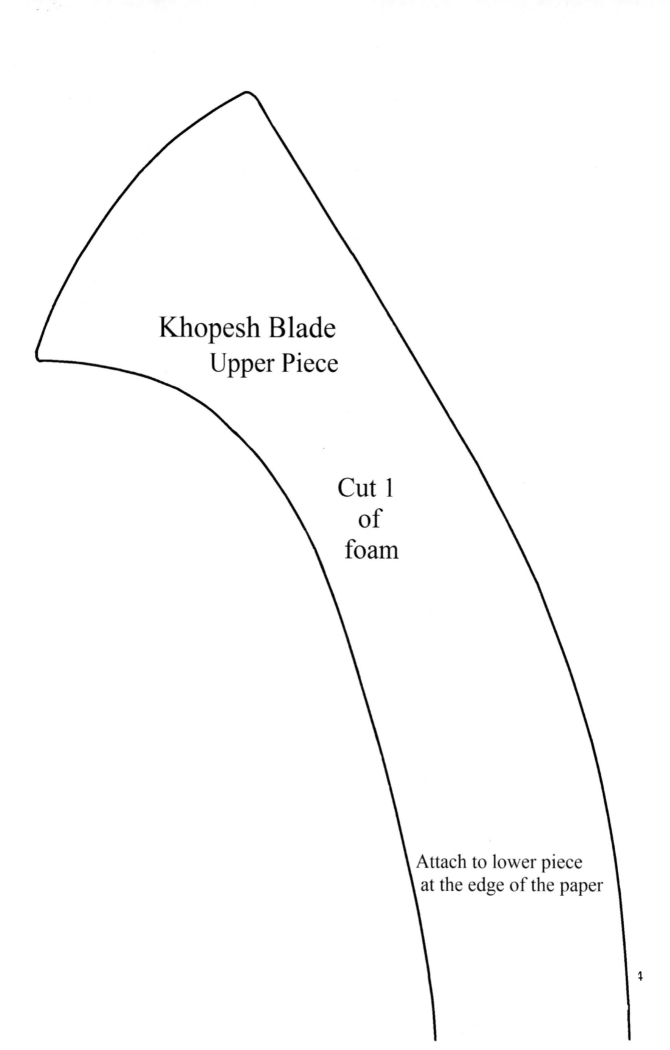

Khopesh Blade
Upper Piece

Cut 1
of
foam

Attach to lower piece
at the edge of the paper

4

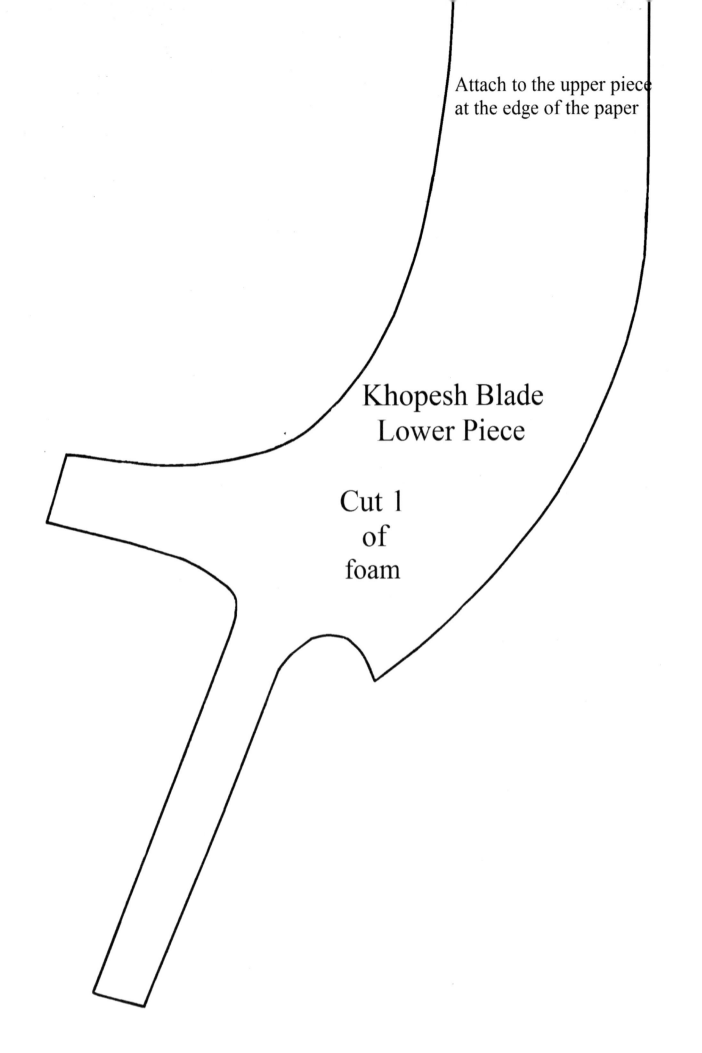

Attach to the upper piece
at the edge of the paper

Khopesh Blade
Lower Piece

Cut 1
of
foam

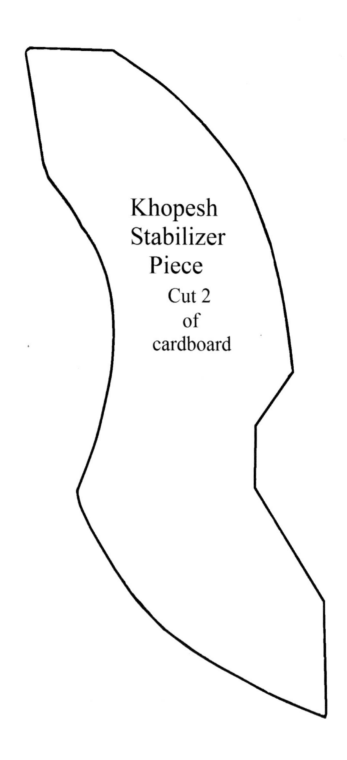

Khopesh
Stabilizer
Piece
Cut 2
of
cardboard

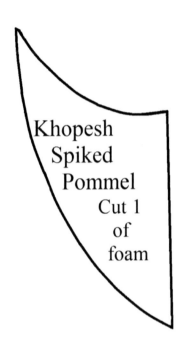

Khopesh
Spiked
Pommel
Cut 1
of
foam

Pharaoh's Belt

Cut 1
of
cardboard

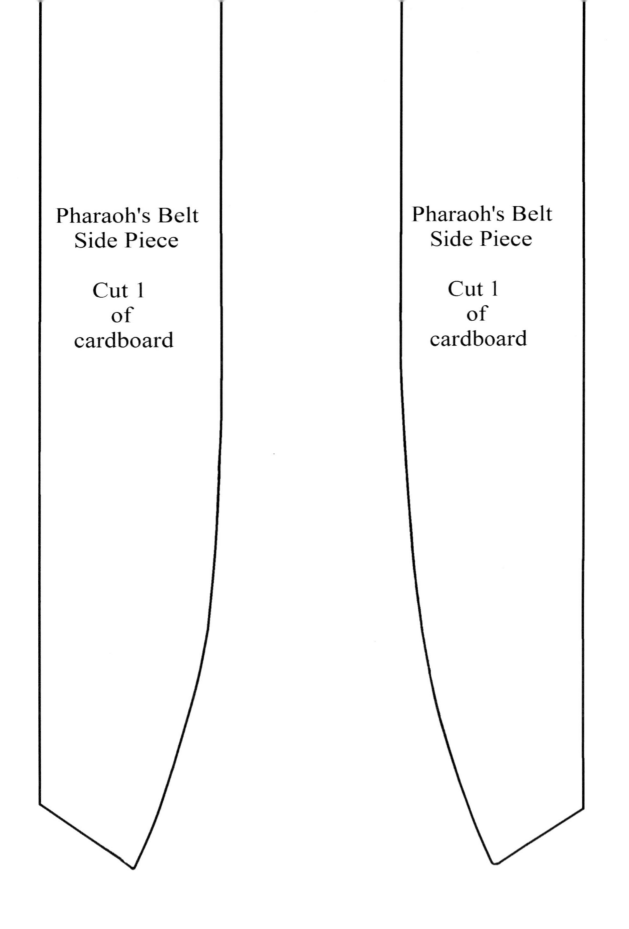

Pharaoh's Belt
Side Piece

Cut 1
of
cardboard

Pharaoh's Belt
Side Piece

Cut 1
of
cardboard

Pharaoh's belt hieroglyph "life"

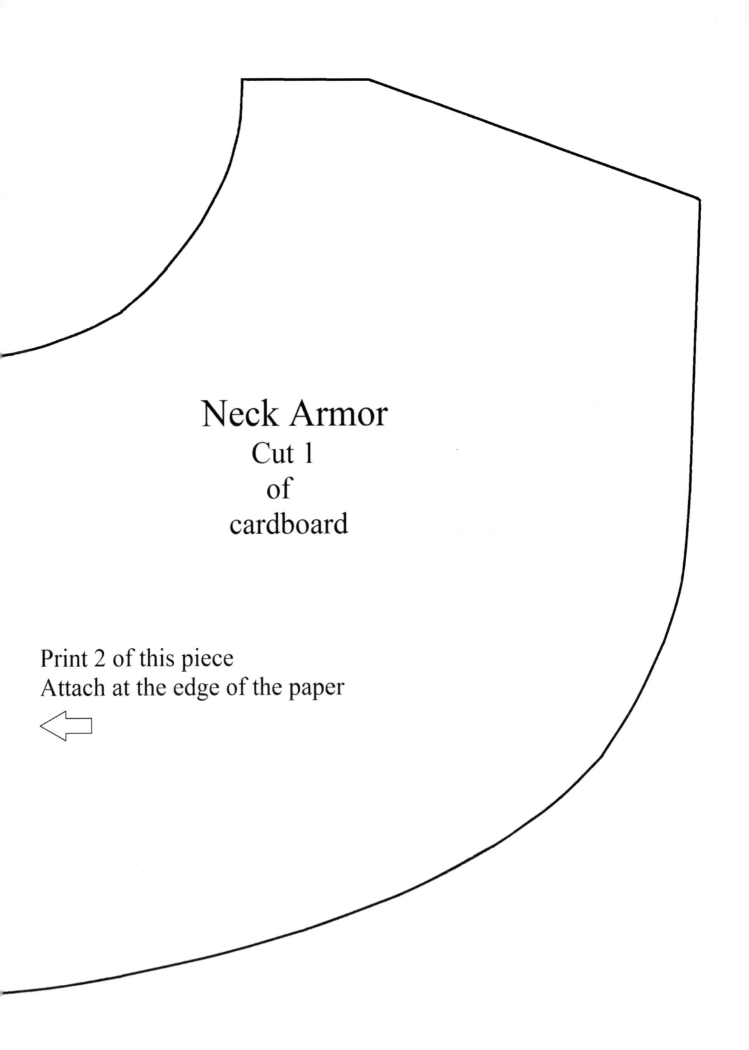

Neck Armor
Cut 1
of
cardboard

Print 2 of this piece
Attach at the edge of the paper

Neck Armor
Shoulder
Extension

Cut 2
of
cardboard

Nemes Cobra Ornament
Cut 1 each
of
cardboard

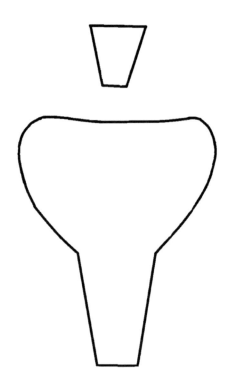

Visit our website
www.warfarebyducttape.com for more
information.

Also available from Warfare by Duct Tape:

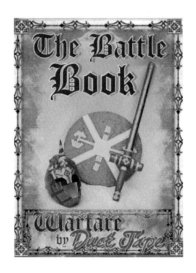

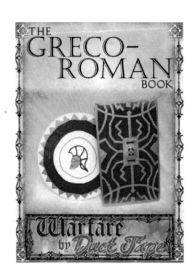

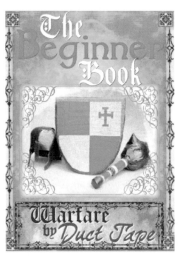

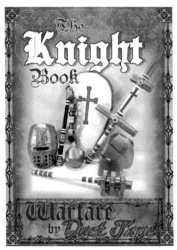

Made in the USA
San Bernardino, CA
15 December 2016